BLACK VOICES ON RACE
NINA SIMONE

by Chyina Powell

FOCUS
READERS®

NAVIGATOR

WWW.FOCUSREADERS.COM

Focus Readers is distributed by North Star Editions:
sales@northstareditions.com | 888-417-0195

Produced for Focus Readers by Red Line Editorial.

Content Consultant: Courtney Patterson-Faye, PhD, Assistant Professor of Sociology, Wesleyan University

Photographs ©: BNA Photographic/Alamy, cover, 1; Chyina Powell, 2; Rene Perez/AP Images, 4–5; Phillipe Gras/Alamy, 7; 3626214 Globe Photos/Media Punch/IPX/AP Images, 8–9; Pictorial Press Ltd/Alamy, 10; Shutterstock Images, 12–13, 18–19, 21, 26–27; Red Line Editorial, 15; AP Images, 16, 25; BJ/AP Images, 22; David Richard/AP Images, 29

Library of Congress Cataloging-in-Publication Data
Names: Powell, Chyina, author.
Title: Nina Simone / Chyina Powell.
Description: Lake Elmo, MN : Focus Readers, [2023] | Series: Black voices
  on race | Includes index. | Audience: Grades 4-6
Identifiers: LCCN 2022012306 (print) | LCCN 2022012307 (ebook) | ISBN
  9781637392690 (hardcover) | ISBN 9781637393215 (paperback) | ISBN
  9781637394212 (pdf) | ISBN 9781637393734 (ebook)
Subjects: LCSH: Simone, Nina, 1933-2003--Juvenile literature. | African
  American women singers--United States--Biography--Juvenile literature. |
  Singers--United States--Biography--Juvenile literature.
Classification: LCC ML3930.S553 P68 2023 (print) | LCC ML3930.S553
  (ebook) | DDC 782.42164092 [B]--dc23/eng/20220310
LC record available at https://lccn.loc.gov/2022012306
LC ebook record available at https://lccn.loc.gov/2022012307

Printed in the United States of America
Mankato, MN
082022

ABOUT THE AUTHOR

Chyina Powell is a freelance writer and editor. She is the founder of both Powell Editorial and the Women of Color Writers' Circle and can often be found with a cup of tea and a book in her hand.

TABLE OF CONTENTS

CHAPTER 1

A PERFORMANCE TO REMEMBER

In 1965, crowds filled a theater. A woman sat at a piano onstage. She had an afro, hoop earrings, and a one-of-a-kind voice. The room went silent. People knew that when Nina Simone began to sing, they were in for a treat.

Simone was a well-known musician. She was known for her unique voice and

Nina Simone stood out for her forceful voice and powerful lyrics.

her live performances. She sang the songs she wrote. She also sang **covers** of others' songs. Many of her covers became more famous than the original versions. One example is her cover of the song "Feeling Good."

"FEELING GOOD"

"Feeling Good" is one of Simone's most famous songs. But she didn't write it. Two British songwriters did. It was for their play, *The Roar of the Greasepaint, the Smell of the Crowd*. The original song was not very popular. Then Simone stepped in. She used a big band. She gave the song a swinging rhythm. The world took notice. Simone released the song during the civil rights movement. It spoke to people's desire to be free.

Simone had a commanding stage presence. People loved to see her perform.

Simone was classically trained. But she wrote and performed songs in multiple **genres**. These genres included blues, jazz, pop, and folk. But Simone was more than a musician. She was also an important voice in the civil rights movement.

CHAPTER 2

A MUSICAL DREAM

Eunice Kathleen Waymon was born on February 21, 1933. She grew up in Tryon, North Carolina. Eunice had a musical gift. She could play by ear at just three years old. That means she knew how to play songs just from listening.

Eunice's parents could not ignore her gift. Her mother was a Methodist

Eunice Waymon was so smart that she skipped two grades in school.

Eunice's mother was a musician, and her father sang and danced. Eunice learned music because of their love for it.

minister. Her father was also a preacher. They allowed Eunice to play piano in their church. Later, she took lessons in classical music. These lessons led her into a musical career.

Eunice went to a **segregated** high school. She graduated at the top of her class. After high school, she wanted to attend a music school. Her dream was to become the first Black classical pianist in the United States. Her teacher collected money to help her pay for college.

In 1950, Eunice took classes at the famous Juilliard School of Music. Unfortunately, racism and rejection kept her from pursuing classical music.

EARLY RACISM

Eunice experienced racism early. At age 12, she performed in a piano recital. Her parents were sitting in the front row. They were told to move for white audience members. Eunice refused to play until her parents got their original seats back. After high school, she applied to the world-famous Curtis Institute of Music. But she was not admitted. She was convinced this was because she was Black.

CHAPTER 3

BECOMING THE HIGH PRIESTESS OF SOUL

To make ends meet, Eunice Waymon taught piano to local students. She also made music with other musicians. Then Waymon heard that night clubs paid well. She began to learn more popular music.

In 1954, Waymon auditioned at a night club in Atlantic City, New Jersey.

Nina Simone's first album included many of her night-club hits.

She wanted to play piano there. But the owner would not hire her unless she also sang. Waymon needed the job. So she started singing nightly at the club.

Waymon knew her mother would not approve of her singing at a club. To hide her job, Waymon used a stage name. She called herself Nina Simone. *Nina* came from the Spanish word for "girl." *Simone* was after a famous actress. Still, her mother found out.

People started to notice Simone. In 1957, at age 24, she was signed by Bethlehem Records. She sang many of the same songs she'd played in clubs. After only two years, she moved to Colpix

Records. Soon, she was performing at major theaters in New York City. She became known for her engaging live performances. Simone rose to the top of the charts for her original songs. She also sang jazz- and blues-inspired covers of other people's songs.

SELECTED COVERS BY SIMONE

1950s	1960s	1970s
"He's Got the Whole World in His Hands" (1959)	"The House of the Rising Sun" (1962)	"Here Comes the Sun" (1971)
"Black Is the Color of My True Love's Hair" (1959)	"It Don't Mean a Thing (If It Ain't Got That Swing)" (1962)	"Angel of the Morning" (1971)
"Cotton-Eyed Joe" (1959)	"Feeling Good" (1965)	"Mr. Bojangles" (1971)
"Summertime" (1959)	"I Put a Spell on You" (1965)	"O-o-h Child" (1971)
	"Strange Fruit" (1965)	"Baltimore" (1978)

Simone toured in the United Kingdom, France, and elsewhere around the world.

Simone performed in multiple genres. But she became known as the High Priestess of Soul. Simone disliked the nickname. She did not want to be tied to one genre of music. She used different styles for different reasons. "Saying what sort of music I played gave the critics problems," Simone once said. "There

was something from everything in there."
She added, "But it also meant I was
appreciated across the board."[1] Folk,
pop, jazz, and blues fans could all admire
Simone's music.

THE POWER OF BLUES

Blues is a poetic form of music. It is based on
the tradition of Black American spirituals. Black
Americans created the blues genre after the US Civil
War (1861–1865). Blues songs focus on sad subjects
and sounds. They are usually about loss or injustice.
But for many Black female singers, they are also
about survival and healing. Blues became popular in
the 1920s. Jazz eventually came out of blues music.
Blues also influenced rock, country, hip-hop, and
R&B (rhythm and blues).

1. "Nina Simone: An Artist's Duty Is to Reflect the Times." *Nina Simone.* Accessed
February 25, 2022. www.ninasimone.com/biography/.

CHAPTER 4

MUSIC AND CIVIL RIGHTS

Slavery in the United States ended in 1865. However, things did not improve much for Black people. Laws in the South made life hard for Black Americans. Black people weren't allowed in public places such as parks and pools. They could be arrested simply for meeting in groups. Then they could be held in jail

Southern laws kept many Black people in forced, unpaid labor even after slavery officially ended.

cells for long periods of time. The laws kept Black and white Americans separate and unequal. Things were not much better in the North.

Black Americans wanted equal treatment. They began the civil rights movement in the late 1950s. In 1963, the civil rights **activist** Medgar Evers was murdered. Months later, the **Ku Klux Klan** bombed the 16th Street Baptist Church in Birmingham, Alabama. The blast killed four Black girls.

These events influenced Simone to join the movement. She wrote songs about the Black experience. Some of her songs were called "protest songs." She also raised

Nina Simone wrote "Four Women" to honor the girls who died in the Birmingham church bombing.

money for civil rights organizations. For example, she supported the Student Nonviolent Coordinating Committee (SNCC). SNCC helped students protest segregation and other forms of racism.

Simone sits with H. Rap Brown, a leader of the Student Nonviolent Coordinating Committee.

Simone said, "I stopped singing love songs and started singing protest songs because protest songs were needed."[2] Simone wrote "Old Jim Crow" in 1964. "Backlash Blues" came out in 1967. Black

2. "How Nina Simone Reinvented Herself After a Rejection from Classical Music Conservatory." *PBS*. January 27, 2021. www.pbs.org.

poet Langston Hughes wrote the lyrics. Simone loved working with other Black artists. She wanted to show her pride in being Black through her songs. She wanted Black people to be proud of who they were.

YOUNG, GIFTED AND BLACK

Lorraine Hansberry was a playwright and friend of Simone's. Hansberry wrote *A Raisin in the Sun*. This famous play is about working-class Black life. She also wrote the play *To Be Young, Gifted and Black*. Simone wrote "To Be Young, Gifted and Black" in memory of her. The song expressed her joy in her Black identity. It became an anthem of the **Black Power** movement. An anthem is an inspiring song tied to a certain group or cause.

THE CIVIL RIGHTS MOVEMENT

The civil rights movement was a fight for equality for Black Americans. It took place in the 1950s and 1960s. Slavery had ended in the United States. But Black Americans still faced **discrimination**.

Black Americans protested in many ways. For example, they held sit-ins. They sat in silence in places they were not allowed to be. Sometimes people attacked the protesters at these sit-ins. Protesters also marched. They gathered in large groups and walked long distances. They showed their determination.

The movement ended in the 1960s with the passing of three laws. The Civil Rights Act of 1964 made discrimination due to race illegal.

Because of Medgar Evers's murder and other atrocities, Nina Simone did not think peaceful protest was enough.

The Voting Rights Act of 1965 improved the opportunities for Black people to vote. The Fair Housing Act of 1968 banned discrimination during the sale and renting of housing. These laws gave Black Americans more rights than they had before. However, many cities took their time in upholding these laws. And problems remain today.

CHAPTER 5

THE LATER YEARS

In the 1970s, Nina Simone took a break from recording music. She felt the message of the civil rights movement had been forgotten. Disco music was gaining popularity. But the genre did not reflect society. Simone felt that an artist's job was to reflect the time she was living in.

Nina Simone did not think the civil rights movement went far enough. She thought the United States had turned its back on Black people.

Simone left the United States and traveled the world. She played in places such as Barbados, France, and Liberia. She never moved back to the States.

Simone eventually returned to recording music. But as her health problems and financial troubles worsened, her popularity decreased. Still, Simone performed until her death. She died on April 21, 2003, after a long battle with cancer. She was 70 years old.

Today, Simone is known for her unique sound. She is remembered for her strong belief in the greatness of Black people. She used music to tell everyone about racial injustice in the United States.

Simone was inducted into the Rock and Roll Hall of Fame in 2018, after her death.

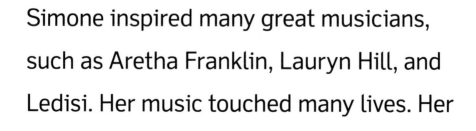

Simone inspired many great musicians, such as Aretha Franklin, Lauryn Hill, and Ledisi. Her music touched many lives. Her legacy continues today.

FOCUS ON
NINA SIMONE

Write your answers on a separate piece of paper.

1. Write a paragraph summarizing the main ideas of Chapter 4.

2. Do you think music is a good tool for fighting for equality? Why or why not?

3. Nina Simone was known as the High Priestess of what genre?

    A. jazz
    B. blues
    C. soul

4. How might Simone's early experiences of racism have influenced her to write protest songs?

    A. Her experiences showed her that Black and white Americans had equal rights.
    B. Her experiences showed her that Black Americans did not have the same rights as white Americans.
    C. Her experiences showed her that equal rights were not important.

Answer key on page 32.

GLOSSARY

activist
A person who takes action to make social or political changes.

Black Power
A movement that began in the 1960s and focused on Black pride and self-reliance as opposed to integration with white society.

covers
New performances of songs that were originally written and performed by someone else.

discrimination
Unfair treatment of others based on who they are or how they look.

genres
Categories of music, such as jazz, hip-hop, and soul.

Ku Klux Klan
An American terrorist hate group that has targeted Black people and other minority groups since the 1860s.

segregated
Legally separated or set apart based on race, gender, or religion.

TO LEARN MORE

BOOKS

Armand, Glenda. *Black Leaders in the Civil Rights Movement: A Black History Book for Kids.* Emeryville, CA: Rockridge Press, 2021.

Braun, Eric. *The Civil Rights Movement.* Minneapolis: Lerner Publications, 2019.

Elizabeth, Jordannah. *She Raised Her Voice: 50 Black Women Who Sang Their Way into Music History.* Philadelphia: Running Press Kids, 2021.

NOTE TO EDUCATORS

Visit **www.focusreaders.com** to find lesson plans, activities, links, and other resources related to this title.

INDEX

Answer Key: 1. Answers will vary; 2. Answers will vary; 3. C; 4. B